NEWS FROM THE VILLAGE

NEWS FROM THE VILLAGE

Poems by

GERALD BULLETT

CAMBRIDGE
AT THE UNIVERSITY PRESS
1952

CAMBRIDGE
UNIVERSITY PRESS

University Printing House, Cambridge CB2 8BS, United Kingdom

Cambridge University Press is part of the University of Cambridge.

It furthers the University's mission by disseminating knowledge in the pursuit of education, learning and research at the highest international levels of excellence.

www.cambridge.org
Information on this title: www.cambridge.org/9781107497771

© Cambridge University Press 1952

First published 1952
First paperback edition 2015

A catalogue record for this publication is available from the British Library

ISBN 978-1-107-49777-1 Paperback

All but two of these items of village news have occurred since the publication of my former collection, *Poems*, in November 1949. Many have appeared in periodicals, and I am grateful to the editors who spared room for them in difficult and crowded times.

G. B.

Autumn 1951

I am certain of nothing but the holiness of the Heart's affections, and the truth of Imagination. . . . The setting Sun will always set me to rights, or if a Sparrow come before my Window I take part in its existence and pick about the gravel. [KEATS, in a letter]

CONTENTS

NO SUMMER YET

We've had no summer yet, they're saying,
And shan't have now, it stands to reason.
Nothing but rain and rain and rain,
In season and out of season.

There's something wrong, without a doubt.
The sun, it seems, is in disgrace.
With all this wild weather about,
He hardly dares to show his face.

But when he does, then as of old
Our drowning world becomes his glass,
Mud and puddle a glitter of gold
More poignant-fair than Eden was.

SEEN FROM A HILLTOP

Now from this island, high
Suspended in the sky,
I see the village below,
Far away, long ago,
A clear leisurely map
Lying in the downs' lap.

The illuminating sun
Lays his gold leaf upon
Cottage and church and farm,
Miniature meadows, warm
Brown acres ribbed by plow,
Haystack and hedgerow,
White roads, clustering timber,
Green, brown, and umber,
The covered Roman camp
Small as a postage stamp,
Far away, long ago.

Look, it is as though
The old cartographer
Having with love and care
Drawn his bright map
Had then fallen asleep,
Unflowing from his hand
The legends he had planned:

'Here dwelleth man.' 'Here browse
By day an hundred cows.'
'Here lovers, paire by paire,
Enjoy the evening aire.'
'In this moon-haunted dale
Plaineth the nightingale.'

OCTOBER

Mellow October,
He turns our green to yellow,
 Our drunk to sober,
Our shrill to bass and cello,

Scatters our leaves,
Tears to wistful tatters,
 Or ties in sheaves,
All (so we think) that matters,

Midsummer glory
Bared in her lusty humour
 To frost and fury,
With Winter the next comer.

Rages October:
Yet in his moody pages,
 Scan we them over,
Sums up the golden ages.

Glummer no story
Than his: yet every comma,
 Dropt seed of glory,
Betokens a new summer.

THE NECKLACE

Rain lingers in rutted lane,
Birds beak at stubble field.
A wide grey sky
Stares at a dead day.

Willowherb, feathery still,
Stands tall and shivery,
His former bravery
No more than a memory.

Dolour for colour. The hedge
Sered with old man's beard,
Where, by malfeasance
Dead, the queen of seasons,

Bereft of hope, look, has left,
Hanging, a lank rope,
Startling to see,
Of berried bryony.

Reckless, she flung her necklace
To hang here shameless, strung
In plain vision
With blood of her passion.

SECOND CHILDHOOD

Crooked as a question-mark,
  See how he sits
Mooning and mumbling
  At sparrows and tits.
Poor old Tom Willow,
  Wanting in wits,
He was once a fine fellow.

At the plow, in the dance,
  He outlasted them all,
Who now shambles along
  At a snail's crawl.
The man of tall tricks
  That gossips recall
Now goes on two sticks.

Time has unsuppled
  That sinewy one.
Dreaming and dribbling
  He sits in the sun
Where now we find him,
  A silly old man.
But the birds don't mind him.

DULL DAY

Why in such weather
Do I find pleasure?
Why joy in a pearl-pale
Dull sky, fine rain filling
Silkenly, quiet as death,
The day's held breath,
Mist veiling the clean
Line of the bare downs,
Trees, as by illness, tranced
Into utter stillness,
A fledgling moorhen's
Weak occasional cry
Forlorn and fond
From her obscured pond?
Why pleasure, why solace,
Why comfort and kindness,
In the taste of the year's
Autumnal tears?

DISTANT SCENE

Man and horse
In the high field
Moving aslant
A silken sky:
Vivid glowing
Arcadian print,
Framed in the eye.

The glitter of gulls
And hovering rooks,
Caper-cutting
Over the plow,
Looks like a scatter
Of burnt paper
And floating snow.

HILL SHEEP IN FLOODTIME

On the slope of a high meadow
Under the hills' shadow,
Secure from flood's rape,
Sheep, each grey shape
Pencilled in golden fire,
Crop their heart's desire.

Nothing those grazers know
Of the drowned land below
Where, bestrewn with sticks
And straw from despoiled ricks,
Liquid sunlight runs
Over the unluckier ones:

Nothing reck of the years'
Inescapable shears,
Nothing of what's to come,
Nor the impending doom
Of lambs, whose meek life
Bedews the butcher's knife.

Sheep, sealed from sorrow,
Take no thought for the morrow.
They know no better than
To enjoy, while they can,
Good food and warm wool.
How stupid! How beautiful!

THE AUCTION

On a day in October the villagers gathered
In the rectory garden, a garrulous company,
To enjoy the remains of the reverend gentleman
Who had married and buried them for half a century.
His dust was dissolving in the church yard.
His ghost pottered in the purlieus of memory.
Remained his garment to be parted among them,
The garment of his spirit, his soul's livery,
Soaked in himself by years of usage.

Warming-pans, water-colours, blankets, bedding,
Carpets, curtains, crocks and casseroles,
A galvanized dustbin, a garden roller,
A portable rosewood desk, genuine antique,
Blunt on the Pentateuch, bound volumes of *Punch*,
A carved walnut stool on cabriole legs,
Mahogany toilet mirror with two drawers,
Prie-dieu chairs upholstered in petit-point,
A set of ivory chessmen and sundry games,
Glass, china, pewter, a useful wheelbarrow,
Brushes and brooms and books various:
These his eyes had looked on, his blunt fingers
Handled, these from his brooding being
Had taken life, character, personality,
That now were items in a printed catalogue,
Yet quick, still, with intangible intimations,
Life in still life, of their bachelor husband.

A raggedry of rooks in the high elms,
Deceived into dreams of domesticity
By the benign unseasonable semblance of spring,
Circled excitedly with raucous caws
Discussing architectural details,
While far below them, on the lank lawn,
Under the golden dome of the wide sky,
The assembled humans, all sorts and sizes,
Craned their necks for a sight of the auctioneer.

Farmers there were, i' faith, and farmers' wives:
Of womenfolk no dearth, I tell you troth.
Trim tweeds and homespun mingled here their lives,
Busy for bargains, gentle and simple both:
Old men and yong, good felawes of all trades
(Dan Chaucer give me grace my tale to tell),
And eke a baronet who with his ladies
Appraised the price of all was there to sell.

And one I was ware of in the living likeness
Of him who was hight/Piers the Plowman,
Honest and earthy, kingly of his kind,
Scored and scarred with centuries of suffering,
Pattern and paragon, mirror and memorial,
Of simple men beseeking a saviour.
Hobbinol the shepherd mixed with his masters,
And Colin Clout, come home from the wars,
With Poitiers pikemen and Agincourt archers

Exchanging chaff with their comrades in khaki,
Appeared from the past in a motley mingle
Of Spenser's pastoral and Langland's England.
Quince the carpenter, Snug and Starveling,
Brave Bully Bottom and Robin Goodfellow,
Lady Hippolyta magnificent in mink,
And the Greek duke and the grave Egeus
Artlessly English as 'a wood in Athens'
Gleamed for a glance on the verge of vision,
To vanish like vapour at rub of the eyes.
And I said to myself, in a moment of musing,
When time and wickedness have done their worst,
The human habitat a ruin of rubble,
The lanes levelled and the fields aflame,
Still shall stir in the memory of man
Living his last in a waste world
The lingering legend of a green island,
A field full of folk, a pastoral peace.

But now, at last, through our crowding company
Ran and rustled a stir of expectancy,
As sitting astride a stool on a table,
Alert for the curt nods of deedy dealers,
Neat Mr Nokes, lifting an eyelid, began
Scattering patter among us like coloured confetti,
While the plump clerk sitting sequacious beside him
Punctually pencilled destination and price,
Lot by lot, of the marketed mystery.

Myself, idly aware, wondered whether
Presently would appear a phantom figure,
And the risen rector's venerable voice,
Testily tell us we were all intruders.
But the bidding went on, seasoned with genial
Jokes from Nokes and the nudging neighbours,
And one by one came under the hammer
Two hundred and forty-five human fragments,
Severed bits and pieces of a long life.
Heaven maintained its immemorial muteness,
And the turning in the tomb made no noise.

THE INNOCENTS

All legs and ears and large inquiring eyes,
Young calves come crowding to the meadow gate,
Eager to greet and nuzzle with soft nose
Good Farmer Herod, master of their fate.

WINTER DAWN

The lantern in the blood burns low.
Winter morning is bleak and grey.
Hedge-birds sit in a sullen row,
Looking dull-eyed at the disarray
Of a lawn mottled with frozen snow.
Loth to believe in the new day,
They huddle together under the grief
Of shrivelled hornbeam sere and brown,
Where aerial spiders, leaf to leaf,
Have spun invisible webs of down
Out of their secret silken life,
For Frost to string his jewels on:
Till the sun, opening half an eye,
Fills with glitter the glassy tears,
Angels invade the desolate sky,
Heaven is with us unawares,
And the sad birds, suddenly spry,
Go to breakfast, forgotten their fears.

COCKCROW

There it goes, the alarum,
Rousing the hennery
At mere threat of daybreak!
Every day of the week,
Hark, at a bleak
Cold crack in the dark,
Before the merrymaking
Of small birds waking
Begins, or stir of furry
Beast in burrow'd nest,
It's the same story.
Wide awake at first shy
Hint of a glint, the king cock
Unfurls, flings high,
His corrugated cry:
'Tantivy, tantivy, tantivy!
Cock-halloo-halloo!
Fire! Murder! Show a leg!
Pull up your socks! Look!
From his sky-covert
The tricksy fox
Is snikkering through
A break in the blue!
Cock-halloo-halloo!'

While he, satanic sentry,
Sounds the loud alarm,

In cottage and farm
By hill and dale
Carrying panic
All over the country,
A dozen cousins' brazen weasands
Echoing the cocky tale,
Meek, his huddled hens,
Bleared eye, pursed beak,
No less scared than bored
By their red, peppery lord,
Sit blinking and thinking,
Thinking but not saying,
'He's at it again!'
And quieter than prayer
The fair, cherub morning,
Heedless of hubbub,
Rides with her sire the sun
Royally on,
To noon's adorning.

THE ALMOND TREE

Calmly this Easter noon my aged friend
Discoursed upon his not far distant end,
Softly decrying, somewhat scant of breath,
The quaint illogical folly of fearing death.

Behind him, through the window of my room,
I saw the incredible almond tree in bloom:
And nodding yes to all he sagely said
I trembled, lest he pause, and turn his head.

THE VIGIL

Not marriages of dust with dust
Can quench the heart's immortal lust,
Nor coil of blood and bone immesh
The living flame in sullen flesh.

Yet not hereafter, not removed
From sensual being known and loved,
Not in a pure idea contained,
Nor in the heaven Plotinus feigned:

Intent, intact, intangible,
There's one within keeps vigil, still
And secret. Not in things of sight,
But in the seeing, lives our light.

DOTAGE

Time was, in lustier years,
The trumpets in the blood
That sang so loud and fierce,
Not to be withstood,
Sealed up his eyes and ears.
Pent in himself he was,
Who now, an aged man,
Enjoys as now he can
The greenness of the grass,
The gleam of sun and rain.

He's one with wren and rook
And small enamelled waif
Adrift in lucid brook
Under a shining sky.
The glad maternal grief
Of the uncurling leaf
Dwells in his doting look.

Living in all he sees
He knows the pilgrim ways
Of birds and honey-bees.
Among the monstrous blades
Lithe ants his errands run.
Quick dragonflies that skim
The willow-shaded stream,

Sharp splinters of the sun,
Describe in darting rays
The zigzag of his dream.

And sometimes at high noon,
Or when the setting sun
Brings heaven to his eye,
In sober Sunday mood
He'll leap into the sky
And ride upon a cloud
The pleasant waters by.
The valley of the shadow
Will hold no fears for him
Among celestial meadows
And lakes of limpid gold.

Waiting his doom at last
He stands before the throne
Where mid a shining host
Sits the Almighty One,
Father and Holy Ghost
And Jesus Christ the son.
Humble yet brave his mien,
For though the heart beat faster
And the knees tremble,
His God is a good master.
So, in a reverent maze,
And pulling at his forelock,

'The name is Caleb Pollock,
I'm not the man I was,
So let thy servant, Lord,
Depart in peace,' he says,
'According to thy word'.

'It's true, more's the sorrow,'
Says Gabriel in God's ear,
'He's not the man he was.
He plowed a straight furrow,
He led his sheep to grass.
But there were times, I fear,
He'd fill himself with beer,
Or wanton with a lass.
He needs a taste of hell,'
Says the angel Gabriel.
But 'Not so fast,' says God.
'Give me your shepherd's crook
And take this harp, old friend.
Here in our heavenly fold
Your sins I'll overlook.
Your ways you will amend
If we forbear to scold.
So, Gabriel,' says the Lord,
'Shut up the fatal book.
And all shall sing with me,
For better or for worse,
Hymn a hundred and three,
Omitting the third verse.'

Then with the holy mirth
Of the angelic song
Echoing in his mind,
Old Caleb wakes to find
Himself once more among
The common things of earth,
His aged heart as young
As when the world began.
Pity then who can
This ancient pensioner,
This multitudinous man,
Freed by the wild frondage
Of musing dotage
From the ego's bondage.

THE BROOK

Here in the shallow brook,
   Under rippling glass
That mirrors the sky's look
   In gleam and shadowiness,
Here with a flowing tide
Flows the enamelled weed
   And the green hair of grass.

The lithe embodied joys
   These lucencies enclose
No rumour troubles. No noise
   Of man their calm can bruise.
The colour of sun and moon
Dropping smoothly down
   Is all their news.

EARLY FROST

Though rime on leaf and lawn
Foretells a frozen time,
Sad skies and daylight brief,
And muted birds at dawn,
Yet Winter's silvery grief,
On barren boughs aglint,
Makes now our desolate earth
Lovely beyond belief.

Not April's growing time
Nor Summer in her mirth
Kindles so keen a glow
As sparkles in his prime,
Nor all their gold and green
Can make a braver show
Than now, austere and cold,
Shines in this naked scene.

SUNSET IN WOODS

As I walked in the wood
   Over frozen ways,
An angel glared
   Thro' skeleton trees,
Red beam of his anger
   Running like a fox
Where rustled the tin-foil
   Leavings of the oaks.

With a ghost-pale moon
   Regarding him,
He spilled his glory
   On the world's rim,
Leaving only his shadow
   To walk the wood,
And the cold air quick
   With beat of his blood.

TSUI CHI

Tired of the long distress,
He rose and went away,
Leaving his earthliness
Alone in its decay.
Crumpled and limp it lay,
The frail apparel shed,
For joy of a new day
Left tumbled on the bed:
As though the risen one,
Freed from his drear night,
With a child's glee had run
Naked into the light.

SILENCE ANSWERS

The flowers fall and the leaves rust.
The bloom and colour of day depart.
Was then that quickness fashioned of dust,
And dust the impetuous human heart?

Silence answers. In storm or calm,
Ebbs to its ending the story of man.
And the etched pattern in a child's palm
Tells more of its truth than doctrine can.

THE TREE

The sunflower and the peacock,
The world-annihilating
Ecstasy of sudden delight
In curved cheek and petal-soft
Warm lips of love,
These visitations and divinings
Can be spoken of.

But the unseen, unmanifest,
Slow-growing tree
Of daily communion
Binding the blind heart
In its spread branches,
The bread we live by, the prose
Profounder than poetry,
This mystery abides
Unregarded, unspoken,
Till life be bereaved
And the heart broken.

SONG

Were this the last goodbye,
Wan hope and trailing wing,
How deep our hearts would sigh,
How fast our hands would cling.
For life's a brittle thing,
A toy wrapt in a shroud,
And love's a blossoming
As brief as it is proud.
So, lips, be not so loud:
The jealous gods are nigh:
Who knows but even now
We breathe our last goodbye?

TRAVELLER'S JOY

Today in the green gloom
    Of an autumnal glade
I found a railway carriage
    Serving for a shed,
Shut in by dripping trees,
    His aspect worn and old,
His rusting wheels sunk deep
    In dark, leafy mould.

Many a metalled mile
    In pride he had raced
Who now in silence stood
    Musing on glories past.
'Sad, are you thinking, friend?
    Not so,' he seemed to say.
'Here is my journey's end,
    Here my traveller's joy.'

SATURDAY CRICKET

Flowing together by devious channels
From farm and brickyard, forest and dene,
Thirteen men in glittering flannels
Move to their stations out on the green.

Long-limbed Waggoner, stern, unbudging,
Stands like a rock behind the bails.
Dairyman umpire, gravely judging,
Spares no thought for his milking-pails.

Bricklayer bowls, a perfect length.
Grocery snicks and sneaks a run.
Law, swiping with all his strength,
Is caught by Chemist at mid-on.

Two to the boundary, a four and a six,
Put the spectators in fear of their lives:
Shepherd the slogger is up to his tricks,
Blithely unwary of weans and wives.

Lord of the manor makes thirty-four.
Parson contributes, smooth and trim,
A cautious twelve to the mounting score:
Leg-before-wicket disposes of him.

Patient, dramatic, serious, genial,
From over to over the game goes on,
Weaving a pattern of hardy perennial
Civilization under the sun.

WINTER ACONITE

The years do not disdain
　　To deck this grave with green,
Nor birds to visit here,
　　Nor sun to shine,
Where, 'in dishonour sown',
　　As on the stone is said,
One misbegotten babe
　　Was put to bed.

So lies, with shame for shroud,
　　Under the robin's perch,
Pillowed in common soil
　　Unsanctified by church,
A small unwanted one:
　　Against whose waking hour
Earth brings, to light the way,
　　The lantern of this flower.

THE BLACKBIRD

This angel, undeterred by cold or rain,
Hymns the eternal morning of the world,
So exiled Adam and his Eve may feign
Their sentence of mortality annulled.

DURFORD MILL

As I passed by Durford Mill,
   The day growing dim,
There they stood, hand in hand,
   Looking down at the stream,
Hand in hand as of custom,
   Kindness, or compassion,
A boy and his sweetheart,
   Drest in an old fashion.

When I gave them good evening
   There came no answers.
Only a sighing and a whispering
   Betrayed the listeners,
And a drawing nearer to where,
   Long centuries past,
In the quiet of the hastening water
   They laid their love to rest.

SUNSET OVER HEATH

Today these eyes have seen,
May they be forgiven,
The holy of holies
And the seventh heaven
Painted on taut silk
By the retired sun
As winter evening came
Invisibly on:
And in the eastern arc
A dim round moon
Lifted her face to look,
Pale from her late swoon.
She and I were alone
With that sublime event,
Her bland orb echoing
The world's wonderment.

NOVEMBER EVENING

Now in November evenings,
   When thick dark falls,
Filling our lanes, and turning
   All mortals into moles,

No moon or stars, no glimmer
   Of lamp, nor means to tell
Hedge from house or haystack
   But by feel and smell,

Glows in my remembering,
   Sounds in my inward ear,
The rattle of dry blown leaves
   In a lit, London square,

And the dim gleam of lamplight
   On leaf-discarding trees
Mingles with urban magic
   These rural secrecies.

SONG

Time's treason all too soon
   Brings April's green to grief,
And makes the rose of June
   One with the fallen leaf,
One with the scattered silks
   That Summer's pride put on,
And the tall towers of Troy,
   And the dust of Babylon.

Yet lingers still her scent:
   The memory and the hope
So mingle and ferment
   In October's cup
That Winter, white with age,
   Half-hearing the shrill noise
Of lusty youth at play,
   Recalls the man he was.

There by the granary doorway,
   Too old for idle tears,
He tells himself the story
   Of the uncounted years,
Recalls of leaping sap
   The fiery pains,
And with the lees of old delight
   Warms his withered veins.

AT PARTING
[after Li Po]

Here in a golden hour
   Morning-shine
And scent of willow-flower
   Mingle with the wine
Which she who comes from Wu,
   Our little serving-lass,
Pours out in measure true
   For each of us.

These gallant lads were up
   At break of day,
To share my stirrup-cup
   And speed me on my way:
And with divided heart
   I in this interim,
While longing to depart,
   Long to stay with them.

Tell me, O eastern tide
   Flowing to the sea,
Which of these longings shall abide
   And go with me?

THE HOMELESS WREN

Rough weather did not daunt this midget wren,
Nor floods and fury quell her active spouse.
With moss and gather'd grass they wove their house,
Unmindful of the busy ways of men,
Who now, so soon as they are settled in,
Made one in mindless faith and brooding joy,
Come with ladder and hedge-bill to destroy
The work of weeks. And all's to do again.

Man's golden eggs grow addled one by one.
Rumour visits the mind in shapes of dread.
But in our veins burns an invisible sun,
And stubborn Life lifts up her drooping head.
All's to do again? It shall be done.
Living and loving cannot be gainsaid.

THE CHURCH MOUSE

Here in a crumbled corner of the wall,
Well stockt with food from harvest festival,
My twitching ears and delicate small snout
And velvet feet that know their way about
From age to age in snug contentment dwell,
Unseen, and serve my hungry nestlings well.

The slanting light makes patterns on the floor
Of nave and chancel. At my kitchen door
God's acre stretches greenly, should I wish
To take the air and seek a daintier dish.
And week by week the shuddering organ mews,
And all my world is filled with boots and shoes.

Sometimes, on Sundays, from my living tomb
I venture out into the vast room,
Smelling my way, as pious as you please,
Among the hassocks and the bended knees,
To join with giants, being filled with food,
In worship of the Beautiful, the Good:
The all-creative Incorporeal Mouse,
Whose radiant odours warm this holy house.

A FIELD IN JUNE

Greed is dumb at sight of so much gold
As these immaculate cups lightly hold,
Nor do we finger with fever'd covetous look
The smooth meandering silver of the brook.
Untaxable bounties entering the mind's eye
From deep meadow and diamond-dropping sky,
Wool-gathering clouds and contemplating trees
Casting palpable shade, those and these
Spell silence, till a skylark, newly risen,
Lets joy and desire out of the dark prison.

ON A LINNET'S EGG FALLEN
FROM THE NEST

Still, in this quiet shell,
Now fallen, now broken,
Singing and delight
Lay sleeping, and swift flight,
And nodding and beckoning,
Coying and pursuing,
In leafy corridors
Lively with interplay
Of sun and shadow:
All here by token.

It wanted but a word,
I think, to awaken
The still bird-being
To singing and flame,
When the Enemy struck,
And the world shook,
And the end came,
No word spoken.

THANKS BEFORE GOING

Now as my dwindling day
Leans into the west,
No light to enliven
The tired guest
But the moon's pale stain
Rising in the east,
What is left but to say
Thanks for the spread feast?

For flower and green leaf,
For daylight and darkness,
And the between hour
When it's as if
The heart listening
At fall of evening
Could hear Time himself
Pause in his hastening:

Thrust of the daffodil
Through winter's crust,
In January, under a sky
Starred and still:
And the astonishment
Of Spring, bringing to bare hedge
The colour and scent
Of a brief blossoming.

What is left but these
Voices and rustlings
Of wild wing'd life
Among darkling leaves?
And friends to remember,
And rare hearts and mellow
Who have gone before me
Where I, soon, must follow.

FALLEN LEAF

His name I do not know.
I saw the fatal frost
Deaden your lantern glow.
But him I did not see.

I did not see the ghost
That pluckt you from the tree
And left you here to rust
Upon the ground below.

Until it fall to me
To render back my dust,
His name I do not know,
His face I cannot see.

THE RETURN

Languid now is the lion of day.
Cold and dearth his pride deny.
Petals fall and are withered away.
The flower returns to its dark joy.